FINISHING LINE PRESS

www.finishinglinepress.com

Porch Light

poems by

Katy Keffer

Finishing Line Press
Georgetown, Kentucky

Porch Light

ACKNOWLEDGMENTS

Many thanks to the online literary journal *Sad Girl Diaries* in which
"Pressure" was published in October 2020.

Publisher: Leah Huete de Maines
Editor: Christen Kincaid
Cover Art: "At Shaker Village" by Ken Keffer ©2018
Author Photo: Kevin L. O'Donovan ©2023
Cover Design: Elizabeth Maines McCleavy

Order online: www.finishinglinepress.com
also available on amazon.com

Author inquiries and mail orders:
Finishing Line Press
PO Box 1626
Georgetown, Kentucky 40324
USA

Contents

For my parents who ignited in me a love of reading and writing.
For my brother with whom I shared a lucky Kentucky upbringing.
And for Kevin who faithfully keeps the porch light on for me.

Red Caboose

An old Kentucky train carries its Red Caboose:
　It chugs and shimmies, rumbles
　　as tumbling thunderclouds.
　　It bends and peers into
　　　turns, sneaks and curves
　　　　where sour bluegrass
　　　　tickles its wheels.
　　　　On this Kentucky country train, Red Caboose trails
　　　　yet is never left behind. I wish
　　　for the sighting of red.
　　My cheers lift, become
　　R O L L e r C O A S T e r s
　as hands reach high to country sky
in slithering waves,
　　　　　　I recall that winding train,
　　　　　　　the wait
　　　　　　　for its Red Caboose.
　　　　　　Its journey long
　　　　　　like waiting rooms
　　　　　　when lights go out,
　　　　　then gone,
　　　　sudden and short
　　　like the end
　　of that stick.
　　What I remember,
　　linger over, ponder
　　now I'm older,
　　　is the taste in the air
　　　as that caboose passed by:
　　　sweet honeysuckle in summer
　　caramel hay scratches on autumn skin
　dusty coughs from winter's fireplace
swaying fields before a spring rainstorm.
　Yes, what I remember,
linger over,
ponder now I'm older,
　　　is:

That charming
Bluegrass country
did not leave me behind.
I am Red Caboose.

Blackberries

I remember summers in Kentucky when June days opened warm and long,
When wasps swayed in lazy swing and bees hummed heavy with heat

where blackberries guarded driveway edges and branches protected ripe flavors
plump and sweet and warm, this all-natural fruit: the big ones are in the back,

I whispered to Brother, and yet, furthest from reach, my purple-red-stained
fingertips at the end of brown arms found their hiding place

on tiptoes my five fingers grabbed their prize. True image of farm to table—
for every three in a basket, one bypassed & rerouted to my mouth— only

what I remember best, the rest joined an after-supper family party
still warm from daytime sun, they melted into vanilla ice cream.

Her Name Was Percy Shades

I hope the crabapple tree on her front hill is still warm from the weight of my small back pressed against its trunk as I counted—*fifteen, fourteen, thirteen, twelve*—in a game of hide-n-seek with my brother. In her back yard, the goats—*eleven, ten, nine, eight*—roam like ghosts and vary, but at one time numbered twenty-one. May the wooden front porch swing still sway, pushed in motion by the laughter of the four of us as the sun made its slow, yellow-orange to pink-purple descent. Long summer evenings brought vanilla ice cream in sugar cones that dripped over pale, sticky fingers—*seven, six, five*—and drops plopped to the wooden boards where our dog Abby appeared at my feet, her brown, black and white fur framing devoted, satin onyx eyes, pink tongue dangling from a smiling mouth. Behind us, Percy's front windows—*four, three*—shimmer into translucent storylines:

Green, red and gold presents unwrapped on Christmas Eve.
Homemade wheat bread and melted butter warmed kitchen corners.
An open spot beside Mom where I dutifully, if begrudgingly, dried dishes.
Blue-lined sheets of math equations waited for me at the dining table.
Nancy Drew books gaped open on the scratchy brown sofa.
Feather-comforter-covered bed where slumber arrived under thunder's rumbling lullaby.

And with all this, I envision a shadow haunts Percy Shades, stands guard 24/7, patrols a long-ago family property overgrown with memories. Is this shadow a raw chunk of my soul? I imagine it sits cross-legged on the slab of concrete beside the water well playing knucklebones as I once did—*two, one*—and looks off into tall maples and oaks draped over a sloping, grassy, central Kentucky knob where deer, snakes, and foxes roam and where wildflowers and poison ivy grow.

And that shadow chortles with a deeper knowing.

A part of me huddles still at Percy Shades, lays flat in her bluegrass, eyes squinting under the sunny country quiet, arms outstretched in a youthful yawn. Oh, what I long to yell: *Ready or not, here I come!*

I Should've Been a Park Ranger

I should've been a park ranger
to smell the trees, and soak up sun
walk next to silent deer, making
the forest my daily run;
instead, the path became four walls,
artificial rays inside gray halls,
sterile air in bare stairwells.

If I had been a park ranger,
discovering arrowheads—
bounties tucked in cool grass—
my lungs would be cleaner,
full of oxygen from tall pines
and no more the nail-biting
weight of a weary coffee break.

I saw a woman hiking through
woods—my woods—reading a book,
not skipping a line in her path,
she let not the air absorb her
nor deer—who patiently ate mere
feet away—distract her. She chose
unawareness in summer woods.

If I had been a park ranger
on high horse, I may have stopped her,
proclaimed wild, colorful words
alive in wilderness all round:
on leaf's pages, in long chapters
of rocks and rivers. The real life
short story lay in summer's sway.

One Beach Run

The beach reaches
spreads wide and far;
Its sand cushions my steps
as I run, seagulls dart left, land gingerly
then skip away from wave's threats.

I am single but not alone.
The ocean as encouragement:
crashing, rolling, blanketing
my path to push me along.
Surfers float in wait
A short distance into sea.
Only sun-browned backs and wet hair
look at me as I pass.

Sun sprinkles through clouds.
The day cool, refreshing for a run.
I continue these steady steps
content to maintain my pace
for what my lungs feel is a long while.

In the last leg, a companion:
rain. It falls steady and sure,
matching my amateur march;
Water rustles from sky
and hushes on land,
my cathartic friend
on this one beach run.

This Little Skeeter

One little skeeter
this morn, hitched a ride
from Carolina to Virginia
on interstate ninety-five
hiding in the seat's underside.

That one little skeeter
showed himself, just one sec,
legs long, heavy and calm
then vanished from sight
eager to avoid
this human's flat palm.

Later, one little skeeter
suddenly floated into view
he must've taken
a four-hour nap—
had he carried cotton
candy pillows and
butter blankets, too?

This one little skeeter
shook his head, declaring
no, I won't let go;
I'll fly to and fro.
Indeed, windows rolled down
were no match for this foe.

Alas, this little skeeter
at mile marker one-five-six
drifted in front of
a travel-weary driver
who ended his multi-state trip.

Pressure

Outside my window, planes land
deafening, their wings too close
to mask the sound. It's heavy
overhead; I gaze, amazed
as hushed yells now bubble up
inside my chest, where he says,
It does no good to complain.

Inside my window, angst builds
like water, warms then boils,
a teapot balloons to pop.
Steady beats the heart, rhythms
of monotonous moments
build into blame. Years pass by.
Is this all there is, she asks.

October Tiptoes

Summer rotates through same bland purpose, cycles on
until, yes, fresh transition turns to October—

when yes, maybe, you now feel lighter in brisk sky
and lift, raise high, floating alongside butterfly

your heart wakens, stomach flutters, skips, then bounces
voice hums, attuned to waves like oceans through tree leaves

orange-red waterfalls rush to tickle your nose
as you peer over cool horizon on October tiptoes

And yes, the season brings love, tilts earth, slows the race
in unexpected turn, lips now brush his soft face.

An Autumn Walk with Friends
(in three haiku)

We walked with Blue Skies,
Orange Leaves, Fire-Red Trees,
Calm, Gratitude, too.

A lone leaf swayed, waved
in one diagonal fall,
landing at our feet.

Then, brown leaf claw surged
skipped past in surprise relay.
Autumn wins again.

Front Porch

At first step, edges
illuminated as
slats of wood
expansive mood
picture-perfect pocket
breath in open yawn
the porch light on
        always, for you

after dark, even
fall or winter, is best
shelter shows itself
as sleek shield
welcome mat gaping
arms encircle, then
welcome you
        always, for you

ribbon of cool silk
is this open river
beckoning embrace
wrap of scarf
warmth that pulls
world's chill, gathers
folds of flowers, fine
vanilla magnolia and pine
sways the swing
        always, for you

vast is language
only we know
outer world before
we cross into
a closed space
of softened souls where

we laugh talk cry and rest,
patiently waiting, the porch
that binds, front and
          always, for you

The Ponti

Our long, green monster,
with a face of embarrassment,
we took a ride
her pointed headlights,
long seats, smells
of age and dust
escaped from inside.

Hovering below view,
we awaited the signal
from Dad once recognizable faces
moved past, no more in sight
of this green monster.

Monsters, however, are not all bad.
Good lurks directly behind faces of shame.
The Ponti took us to the drive-in,
hid Christmas presents in her trunk,
protected Abby—our new brown-eyed puppy,
replaced the truck after the crash.
She became trusted vehicle for us all.

Snow Day

Awake in joyous occasion, when finding—
    walkways covered
    driveways closed
    families stranded
Then three words: "School is cancelled"
    like sugar on lips
    money in the piggy
    a new toy
Brother and I celebrated, discarded pajamas
    no school bus ride
    homework forgotten
    friends by phone
Outside we go where clouds mirror billowy snow
    footsteps lost
    swallowed in crunches
    piles of frozen white feathers
Runny noses unnoticed, damp sleeves rub faces
    an orange saucer hovers
    bottoms cold on thin plastic
    we rush all the way down.

Fire Chief

With crackling breath
and smoky sighs,
warmth flows over my face.
Heat reaches, meets my watchful eye.
A dance begins, sways
crackles back and forth
orange flames against dry wood
translate into Fire Chief's language
pops, hisses, snaps,
bounce over solid steel.
The dance continues—in flames now—
circles and hugs smother wet snow.

Sweet Salute

Moon casts her squinting gray eye,
a pale cape where bumblebees lie.

Black and yellow backs dulled from sight,
at midnight, they rest from flight.

Rose trees, stiff from winter's doze,
quiver and scatter dreary clothes.

First morning light removes Moon's chill,
breathes life to the daffodil.

The bright Moon will rest for now,
marching with hope, taking her bow.

Spring's perfumed promise lifts its nose,
sweet salute to budding rows.

You Have Worth

Too many years in the making
too many to recall or count
but yes, today
    one random day
I bade farewell. I quit my job.

So, I go outside, take a walk
let the pollen-yellow bright trees
and the impermanent presence
of earth, light, air, lazy breezes
ground me again, bring me back home.

I see a silent chickadee
hiding tucked under leaf cover
within tree's early canopy
of Spring's shade umbrella.

He watches as I pass, eyes closed
as slits, his neck follows my route.
No singing, no flutter of wings.
Wait now, was that a silent nod
of black-eyed tuxedo courage?

Indeed, why yes, I meet it next

Encouragement in bright blue chalk
Words draped across the path, my path.
I must cross over.
I must see the big blocks
Letters which shout, YOU HAVE WORTH
precisely what I need right now.

How Now

How is it that a heart
hurts so much, constricting
your chest, grinding your stomach,
pushing tears from your eyes
which turn red and then, why then
the ache in my head?
I think I know how,
    now.

It is because the heart absorbs
so much love, so large a sum of
memories happy and sad, and dreams
for future ones too, that
when it seems those will be gone,
when the void occurs, as if the
love in your heart will disappear.
that is how the heart can hurt,
    now.

But it won't disappear, that love,
an intangible, humming energy
upon which we place no finger;
it cannot disappear, it does not;
it remains in us. That's how,
    now.

The memories persist; the heart becomes
whole again, perhaps
with less physical pain,
and fewer tears shed. Instead,
tears become kisses of hope on our cheeks,
memories, whispers walking the streets.
This is how

Now, we breathe again;
lift our faces and
grow from where we've been.
Anticipate strength in where we'll roam, and
lift clear eyes to move forward once more.

Azalea's Promise

Oh, there are those days
when you wish for rain to stay indoors,
instead, some force pushes you out of doors.
Your hands seek Earth, dirt showers fingers
kneads crumbly layers humming
with busy ants and jelly-brown worms;
you forge a new pathway.
Therapy is a garden where cries dissolve into
birdsong and tears sprinkle cool refreshment.

Age emboldens pink and white azaleas
now three times their early size. How do they flourish
in this small enclosure? Is it soaring soaking sun
or morning's waking breath blowing
brilliant dew drops that turn them rich? Perhaps—
they thrive by caress of sour compost,
yawn in delight at flower's flutter.
Their therapy is growth, roots seeping deeper,
stretching further into underground.

And you, too, flourish as years layer,
then lengthen twilight's lines. There,
you peer into azalea's promise
which softens into snowy silk
and pulses heartbeat pink.
Therapy is azalea's gaze
nodding, resting, loving
Earth. In this garden, her promise
forges today's faithful breath.

Nature's Mother

She is laughter on a ledge
balancing between land and air,
balancing between assured and forgotten.

Her stride—long and vast—casts sultry
shadows over dry country fields,
shadows over warm, washed-out city sidewalks.
Change arrives: she bounces, floats,
points toes to cinnamon and pepper piles
of chocolate, orange, and lemon leaves.
Fingertips reach to pale-faced skies,
fall through drifting white cotton,
shiver into feather blankets of frost.
There, she huddles next to crackling whispers,
tales of days past sting her face,
brush her eyelashes, warm her weary shoulders,
underneath star-like snowflakes.
Eager for energy, she stands still, rests;
In a yawn, she opens arms wide,
signals lingering, pause, reflection.
And then, a jump rope turns free;
she skips and hops, twists and turns
as sun-swept green lawns sway in a fresh day
as sounds of forests and streets weep
                with seasonal delight.

She is laughter on a ledge
teetering between kind and cruel,
teetering between song and storm.

Bird's Balm

Bluebirds eavesdrop as my lips long
for a whistle of sudden song.

Waters tap dance sparrow's hello,
trickling morse code at pond's shadow.

Melody sounds, wrens dip down.
Trees flicker sunlight all 'round.

Blades of grass beckon *come here.*
Black crows pass, surface my fear.

Nature's mirror reflects my face,
a line shimmers: slow, wet shoelace.

Birdsongs stop, my lips untwist—
I sigh; birds sit. Tears persist.

Then, wild notes soar, rise in embrace
my cheeks, my eyes, my heart—kind grace.

Goldfinches sing, spring to fly
as breath flutters by, tears dry.

Sky sprinkles leaves, alights bright calm
when sprightly song becomes bird's balm.

If It's a Diamond You Seek

If it's a diamond you seek,
look to rivers of tulips
swaying cups of pink and red
nature's gems across your lips.
The diamonds you seek lay tucked
hidden in sweet March dirt; they
whistle a cool blowing breath
whisper words to heal old hurt.

If it's a diamond you seek,
find it in morning's kiss, when
dew drops are pockets of sun
along earth's raised fingertips.

These blades of grass cry happy
joy for the sparkle of spring
love: it quivers, then shivers
dances in pastures that sing!

Shifting

Why do I miss what I have known
but a week?
Since the first steps for apartment hunting
to a sampler of beer and chips, then coffee.

A roller coaster, twists and turns,
spanning seconds and days.
The weather shifted;
maybe the world is messing with us.

I don't want the sadness
on my doorstep;
Nor the loneliness
at my table.

Instead,
I want new lands
with water to touch
and shade to hide under

where silent hay bales stand watch,
protectors in fields of wheat:
shimmering,
swaying,
covering us as we look from rain clouds
into blue skies.

Dear Kevin

You are sunshine in thunderclouds
First sip of coffee on Saturday morn
Lemon fresh clean sheets,
Soft spring breeze after a long winter
Melted butter on sourdough bread
Warm fire and hot chocolate on a snow day
First sight of the ocean after too long away
Perfect precious single snowflake found in my palm
Quiet place when tired and lonely
You are love greater than all my favorite things

Escape Artists

This poem is about you, dear tulip, not clouds or wind or sky; tomorrow's downpour of nourishment arrives through open tree limbs where you are crouched, an offering tucked in damp dirt of random pose. Today's triumph began months ago with crinkly, tissue-wrapped bulbs, soft sandpaper laughter in late autumn leaves. You slept snuggled underneath blankets of midnight cool dirt, alive with worms and stones; you lay below flakes of frost turned to spongey layers of snow; you waited like knucklebones scattered in precise rows pointing, ready for sun-warmed cloaks of winter's final breaths. Worry stretched long then; when you (and I) were entrenched: captives.

And yet,
you and I break free
    from dizzying dreams of drunken cold
bodies sway in earthy vapors of new soil:
    there is a rush of lemon, tangy metal, full
of forgotten safflower seeds
    bitter and dark from winter's doze, moist
acorns split open to swallow sun's heat;
    crisp pine needles sprawl
as evergreen guardians of earth's underground.

You and I march together—
your footfalls lengthen, lean
flowers of yellow, pink and red;
my footprints sink in
fresh surrender, a mold in wet sand.
    We grasp moment's forever.

This poem is about us, nature's explorers of Spring, plucking pathways to strum easy melodies. Rest a while in my hand—soften spots of age and lines of anxiety—and become the glow of healed hearts. Satin petals float like fragile feathers tickling the season. Life alights in serendipity of hummingbird: its emerald return a promise; its dazzling presence a blossom of hope.

And thus,
      you and I bloom,
      escape into art.

Let's Fly

Oh, to fly then hover alongside the other
geese who skim diamond-sprinkled water,
flowing glass that breaks then shakes
winter's mood; Spring lingers longer now.
Following a wish to fly, my destination:
this choppy river, a curving string where long wings

lift

       then

                                    again.

          fall,

                  lift

             then

Arms and wings lie flat and thin.
Where do geese end and I begin?
Outstretched necks slice silent air pockets
inches above water where no wind reigns.
A smooth race for wide horizon, we glide
within a pause, between one day and was,
   is only now.
As water's glistening cheer speeds by,
we relish this ride, side by side.

Oh, to fly and hover alongside the other
loyal geese leading, we slow to near halt:
wind's wall, its face a shifting menace. A glance
left then right—do we continue or alight?
With little time to decide, they chide this gusty foe.
The geese choose forward, honking their strength,
surpassing the invisible curtain, they fly.
   And so must I,
               so must we all.
Oh, to fly ever steady alongside each other.

Where do geese end and I begin?

Friends

One bright red cardinal
nods, greets
one dirt brown sparrow
who dips, meets
cardinal's eye. They stand,
perch shoulder to wing
atop the fence
pleased—in their bird-like way—
to find food in this winter-ready
backyard, waiting
acutely aware of snow
set to fall in the coming hours.
Friends, these birds are,
after all.

Beings We Remain

And with barely a clap or snap
of her fingers, the New Year spoke
in damp cover with bitter mouth
at the one left behind. Tis now
a start, a step across silence.
Bridges and walkways
wait, then anticipate
renewed force of life only to
blend, merge, then mend
sorrows of long ago into
laughter like rainwater into
beings we carried then into
beings we remain, even now.

For the Love of Goat's Milk

I would love to taste again that first youthful gulp of goat's
milk, recall my original reaction to its sour sweetness. I
would like to know if the fresh, off-white liquid our milk
goat Jenny produced washed over my tongue and throat
as sun-warmed hay and honey. I long for the reminder of
molasses, lemons, and bright summertime grass.

What I'd give to be seven again, to imprint the scents, the
heavy and thick texture of this goat's milk surrounded by the
rustle of weeds in the woods around Percy Shades. I would
love to better remember:

the curve of the gravel driveway,
the cluster of tall trees in the yard,
the texture of siding on our small farmhouse,
the creak of wood under the front porch swing,
the number of steps my feet needed between the front yard
crabapple tree and back porch light.

But most of all, I'd love to hold a glass of her milk in one
hand and run the other along Jenny's nose as her brown
eyelashes swoop shut in the blissful moment that manifests
from sunshine, youth, and Kentucky country air.

Katy Keffer writes poetry, nonfiction and fiction inspired by her childhood in Kentucky, the natural world around her, and random daily life. When not writing, she's reading submissions as Managing Editor for the online literary journal *The Bluebird Word*, which she founded in February 2022 to promote writing from emerging and established writers worldwide. She has an MBA from UNC-Wilmington, an MFA in Writing from Lindenwood University, and over twenty years as a federal employee in the Washington, DC area. Some of her work appears in the 2023 and 2024 editions of *Freshwater Literary Journal*, as well as *A Plate of Pandemic, Hare's Paw Literary Journal, The RavensPerch,* and *Sad Girl Diaries.* She currently calls Virginia home.

www.ingramcontent.com/pod-product-compliance
Lightning Source LLC
Chambersburg PA
CBHW022045080426
42734CB00009B/1241